Forex Swing Trading

The most profitable swing trading strategies for trading
forex

Effectively following the price action and market
structure

Abraham Robert. C

In order to say thank you for purchasing this book, I offer the below video course and more to you as a token of appreciation

**Find the Link to the bonus video courses at the end of the book**

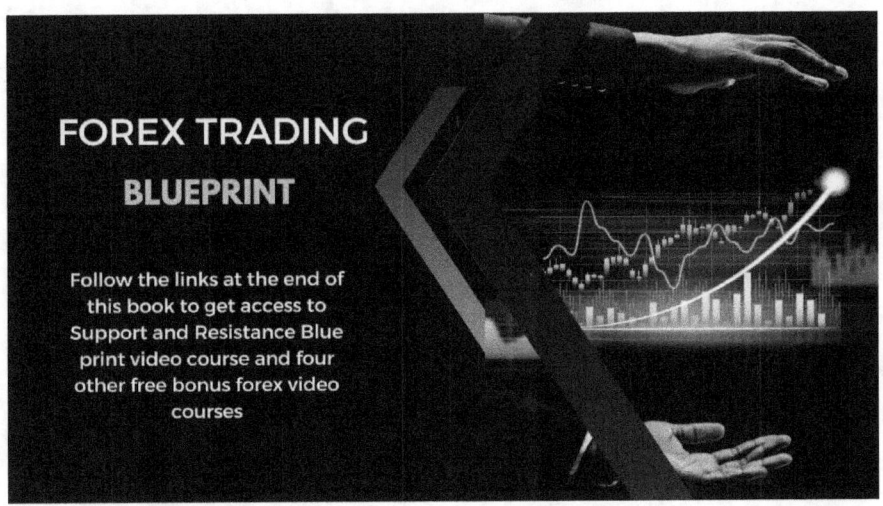

FOREX TRADING
BLUEPRINT

Follow the links at the end of this book to get access to Support and Resistance Blue print video course and four other free bonus forex video courses

TABLE OF CONTENT

CHAPTER 1

OVERVIEW OF SWING TRADING

Swing trading is a trading strategy that aims to benefit from market "swings" in direction over the short to medium term. Swing traders seek to benefit handsomely from intermediate-term market patterns.

Swing trading is a trading method that is in between position trading and day trading.

Position trading is a long-term approach where deals may be kept for many months or years, in contrast to day trading, which is holding trades within a single day or trading session. Trades are kept for a few days or weeks during swing trading.

Technical and fundamental analysis are used in swing trading to determine market direction and the best times to enter and leave the market.

There will be several intraday price variations while the deal is being executed, thus patience and composure are required while using the swing trading approach.

Another adaptable tactic that works in most markets is swing trading. Swing traders have the ability to trade assets with larger spreads or lower liquidity due to their relatively substantial profit objectives.

Swing trading is essentially a strategy that looks to predict a future market price change and seeks to benefit handsomely if that move occurs. In the market, swing traders use a range of tactics. Reversal trading, retracement trading, and breakout trading are a few of the most popular.

The world's biggest financial market is FX. Since there are often plenty of swing trading possibilities across major, minor, and exotic currency pairings, this is most likely the finest market for swing traders. Every day, a variety of variables impact the prices of currency pairings, which presents a wealth of chances for swing trading.

Swing trading tactics may be used on minor and exotic currency pairings as well, since large price objectives can counteract the effect of comparatively bigger spreads. Although many traders like major currency pairs, such the EUR/USD, because to their smaller spreads.

Every trading strategy has benefits and drawbacks, and a vast array of them are regularly used in the forex market. Certain approaches have a stronger track record than others in terms of outcomes.

Forex traders have shown a significant basis of support for swing trading. Given that positions are often maintained for much longer than a day and not simply overnight, it is generally considered a basic kind of forex trading.

This is due to the fact that the majority of fundamental traders, also known as fundamentalists, are swing traders who base their decisions on fundamentals that often need several days or longer to produce significant price swings necessary to produce a profit.

As swing trading tactics proliferate in the forex market, it's critical to comprehend everything that goes into them in more detail.

Benefits of Trading Swings

Reduced time commitment

Swing trading requires a less time commitment than day trading. Watching charts on a daily or 4-hour period is all that swing traders need to do since they mostly employ technical analysis. They don't have to spend all day observing their charts or keeping an eye on smaller chart periods' price movement. For this reason, swing trading is very accommodating, especially for traders with day jobs.

Reduced stop-losses

Your stop losses are tiny while swing trading, particularly when compared to longer-term positions. For instance, a swing trade's stop-losses based on a standard four-hour chart may be 100 pips, whereas a stop-loss based on a weekly chart and the whole position might be 400 pip.

In light of this, swing trading enables you to choose for huge bets as opposed to those that often involve low leverage and longer time horizons.

Easier movement in line with the markets' natural flow

In the best-case scenario, you may benefit from increasing prices in a bull market and decreasing prices in a bear market by using the appropriate swing trading method. Swing trading allows you to move with whatever the forex market has to offer as it doesn't tie you into any certain market.

Greater Profit on Individual Trades

Swing traders' constant goal is to benefit handsomely from medium-term market movements. This entails searching the market for transactions with compelling risk/reward ratios. This often leads to deals that provide enormous gains in relation to the risks incurred in making them.

Trading professionals can exclusively rely on technical analysis

Technical analysis plays a key role in swing trading methods. Because only very basic fundamental research is needed to take advantage of the finest trading chances in the market and use the best swing trading tactics, this streamlines the trading process.

Disadvantage of Swing Trading

Exposure to price surprises overnight and weekend

Swing transactions usually take place over the course of a weekend or overnight. This puts traders at risk for things like price gaps or significant news and events that might occur on the weekends or after business hours. Such occurrences may cause swing trading in the market.

It's Hard to time the market

Technical analysis is a key component of swing trading as it helps predict market fluctuations in medium-term prices. But given that price behavior may be erratic and turbulent in the near term, market timing is a highly challenging task—even for seasoned traders.

In the next chapters, we'll examine many useful tactics and top indicators for market swing trading.

CHAPTER 2

USING SUPPORT AND RESISTANCE LEVELS IN SWING TRADING

These levels are an ideal representation of how the market's forces of supply and demand work to decide the price of financial assets.

Prices will often decline until supply cannot keep up with demand; this is the point of support when prices are most likely to rise. On the other hand, if supply surpasses demand, the price will increase and reach the resistance level, from which a decrease in price is anticipated.

When the market rebounds off support zones, swing traders often try to initiate buy transactions.

When buying a trade, the stops are set just below the support zone, while the profit objectives are close to the resistance zone.

Similarly, when the price rebounds off the resistance level, sell transactions will be made. After that, stops will be positioned slightly above the resistance zone, and profit targets will be close to the support zone.

When swing trading off support and resistance levels, it's critical to keep in mind that the levels take on a different function when price violates them. For example, a support line becomes a new level of resistance if the price crosses it.

What Are Resistance and Support

Support and resistance levels are horizontal price levels that, on a price chart, often link price bar highs to other price bar highs or lows to lows.

When a market's price movement reversals and shifts, leaving behind a peak or trough (swing point) in the market, a support or resistance level is created.

As we can see in the chart below, support and resistance levels may define trading ranges. They can also be seen in trending markets when a market retraces and leaves behind swing points.

Until the price naturally breaks through these levels of support and resistance, it will often respect them and limit price movement.

The creation of support and resistance levels in a market may also be attributed to trend swing points.

When a market trends, it retraces its steps, creating a "swing point" in the market that appears as a trough in a downtrend and a high in an uptrend.

When price breaks over prior peaks in an uptrend and then retraces back down to test them, the old peaks often serve as support. The converse is true in a downtrend; once price breaks through the previous troughs and retraces back up to test them, it usually acts as resistance.

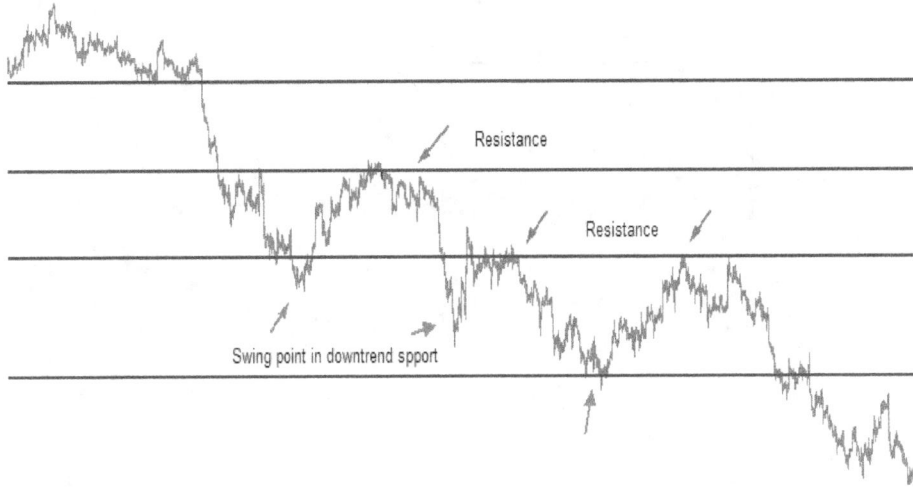

Swing Trading Breakout

When entering the forex market at the beginning of a trend, aggressive investors use breakout trading, another swing trading approach. Breakout trading may be used as a method for significant price moves and volatility expansions, all while reducing risk when done correctly.

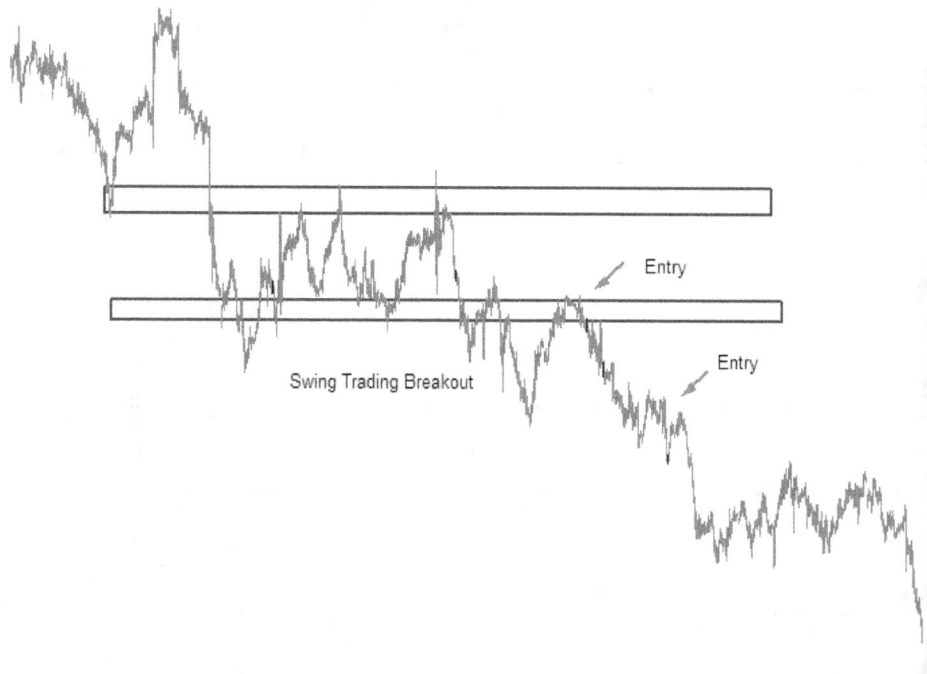

Swing Trading Breakout

When a currency crosses a line of support or resistance, it is said to have broken out. Usually, high volume and higher volatility follow. Then, when a profit opportunity presents itself in either direction, traders will often purchase the asset.

Retracement

A retracement is a little shift in the general direction of a price, as opposed to a reversal. It usually only lasts temporarily and doesn't always portend a change in the general direction of the trend. The trend that was previously in place should continue when a retracement finishes.

Retracement trading is a profitable swing trading method that entails determining the general direction of the price trend and entering the market after the trend has reversed.

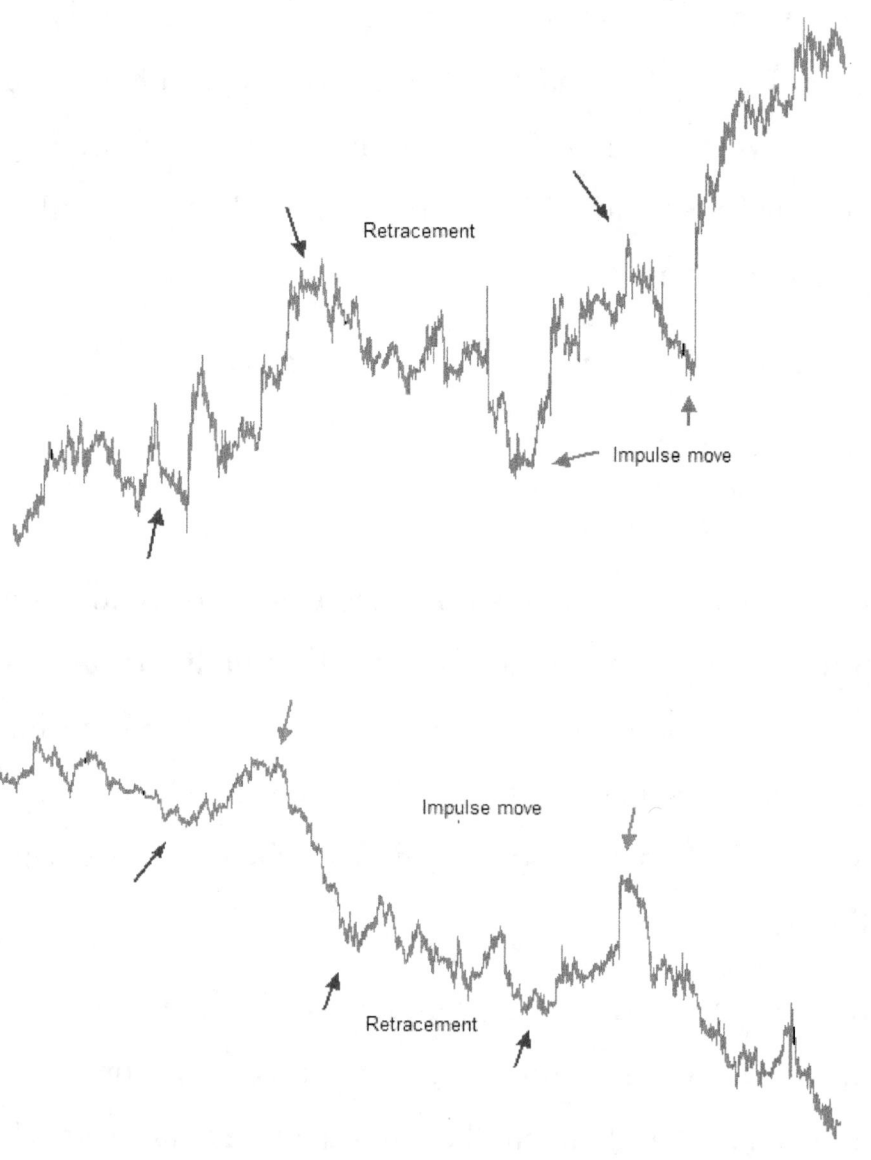

CHAPTER 3

USING CHANNELS FOR SWING TRADING

For assets that are significantly moving, swing trading across channels is particularly advantageous. Finding an item that is significantly moving inside a plotted channel is essential for successful swing trading. In essence, channels are parallel trendlines.

It's crucial to only place trades in the direction of the primary trend while using channels. For example, if an asset is heading downward, it is best to wait to issue sell orders until the price reaches the channel's upper line. The channel's bottom line might then be the price goals.

Only when the price is confined inside the channel can swing trades be executed.

Price breakouts from the channel indicate the emergence of fresh market conditions, necessitating the need to adjust your approach or draw new lines.

Trading using channels

Finding a market that is showing a strong trend and trading within a channel is necessary for this swing trading method.

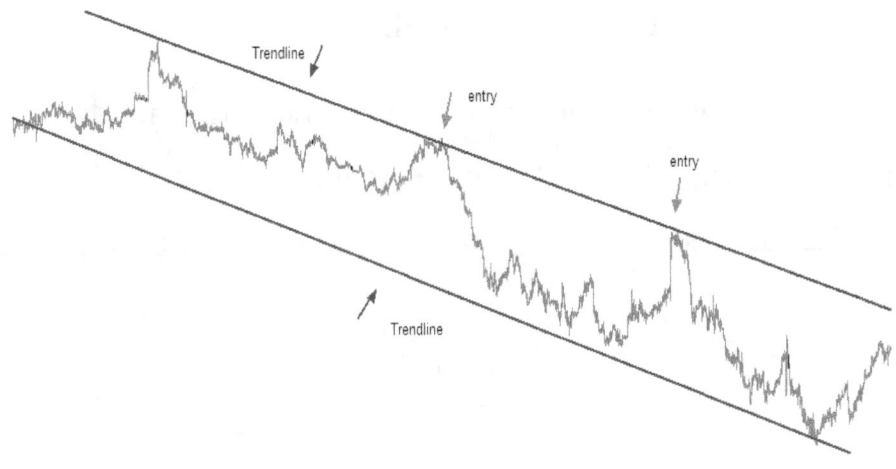

When the price rebounds back off the top line of the channel, you should think about initiating a sell position if you have drawn a channel around a negative trend on a market chart. It is crucial to trade with the trend when swing-trading using channels.

In this case, when the price is down trending, you would only look for sell positions until the price breaks out of the channel and moves higher, signaling a reversal and the start of an uptrend.

Once three bottoms can be linked to the trendline, a trendline is established for the sake of this method. After that, the trendline is stretched to the right.

All three lows are the only places where the trendline must connect. It is not required to link all three of the precise low spots.

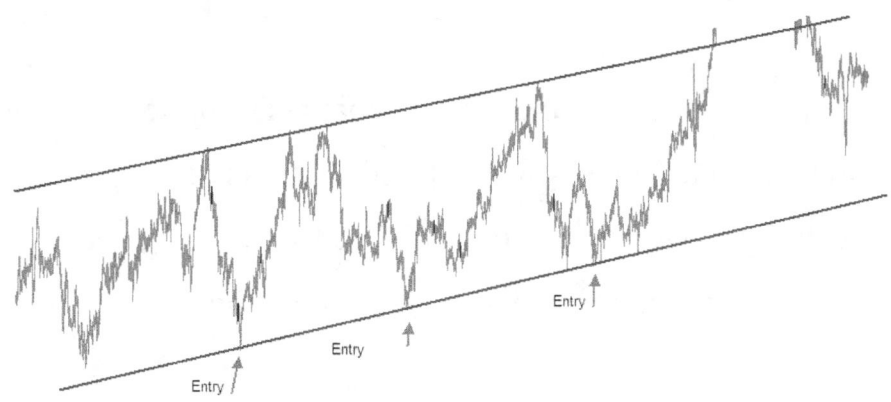

After three swing highs, an upper trendline is established. Along the top of the swing highs, a line is drawn and stretched to the right.

Once again, just make sure that it is touching each of the three high spots, and it simply has to be close by. It's not necessary to go directly along the peaks.

Where and How to Get into a Trend Channel Trade

Buying close to the trend channel's bottom is the fundamental tenet of the trend channel swing trading technique. However, you will fast lose a lot of money if you do it without considering any other factors.

A signal indicating that now is the right moment to purchase must appear close to the trend channel's bottom. We refer to this as a trade trigger.

Waiting for a consolidation in the vicinity of the trend channel's bottom is my preferred entry strategy. When price goes mostly sideways for more than a few days, it is called a consolidation.

The trendline of best fit should be close to, or perhaps slightly below, where the consolidation takes place.

Purchase when the price crosses above the consolidation's high point.

Occasionally, a consolidation occurs in the vicinity of the channel's bottom; other times, it does not.

BEST ENTRY POINT FOR UPTREND

CHAPTER 4

UTILISING CANDLESTICK PATTERNS FOR SWING TRADING

Technical analysis plays a major role in swing trading. Additionally, employing candlestick patterns for raw price movement research is a fantastic method of doing technical analysis. Candlesticks may create patterns in the market that, when closely observed, can provide important clues about price movement.

In particular, continuation and reversal patterns are sought for by swing traders. After a time of consolidation, continuation patterns like wedges and flags signal that the price of an asset is prepared to restart the dominating trend.

Finding effective entry and exit opportunities is essential for swing trading.

An important tool for giving traders a visual picture of market emotion is technical analysis. Candlestick patterns are one of the most often used techniques in technical analysis. whether deciding whether to join and exit deals, traders may use these patterns to get insight into market movements. Traders may use a range of candlestick patterns to recognize trends and forecast future price changes.

Some of the most often used candlestick patterns for swing trading are listed below.

Bullish Engulfing pattern

A tiny bearish candle is followed by a huge bullish candle that engulfs the preceding candle entirely to produce this pattern. This pattern is often used by traders as a buy signal since it is a reliable indicator of a trend reversal.

Entrying a swing trade from a bullish engulfing

Bearish Engulfing Pattern

This pattern, which is the reverse of the bullish engulfing pattern, arises when a big bearish candle completely engulfs the preceding little bullish candle. Traders often use this pattern as a sell signal since it is a reliable indicator of a trend reversal.

ENTRY ON A BEARISH ENGULFING

Hammer

When a bigger bullish candle follows a smaller one with a lengthy lower wick, a hammer pattern is created. This pattern is often seen as a buy signal as it suggests a possible trend reversal.

ENTRY FROM A HAMMER CANDLE

Shooting Star

The reverse of a hammer pattern, a shooting star pattern is created when a bigger bearish candle follows a smaller one with a lengthy upper wick. This pattern is often seen as a sell signal as it suggests a possible trend reversal.

For example, when a bearish wedge appears on a chart of a market that is heading downward, it indicates that the price is likely to continue falling and sell orders should be placed.

However, reversal patterns like head and shoulders and double tops suggest that the present trend's strength is waning and that the price will probably shift directions.

Trading professionals may find high probability swing trading chances in the market by analyzing price movement using candlesticks.

CHAPTER 5

USING MOVING AVERAGE CROSSES FOR SWING TRADING

Plotting the average price of an item over a certain period of time is how moving averages are known to smooth out price movement. For example, the average price over the last 20 days may be shown by plotting a 20-period moving average on the daily chart.

In order to identify the current price fluctuations in the market, swing traders often blend numerous moving averages. For example, a 5-period and a 13-period moving average may be used simultaneously. The shorter-period moving average will respond to current prices more quickly than the longer-period moving average when several moving averages are used.

To identify the finest chances in the market, swing traders keep an eye out for crossings of the moving average. Sell trades may be made in the market if, for example, the price has been trending upward and, after a time of losing momentum, the 5-period moving average crosses below the 13-period moving average. This would suggest that a downward swing is underway.

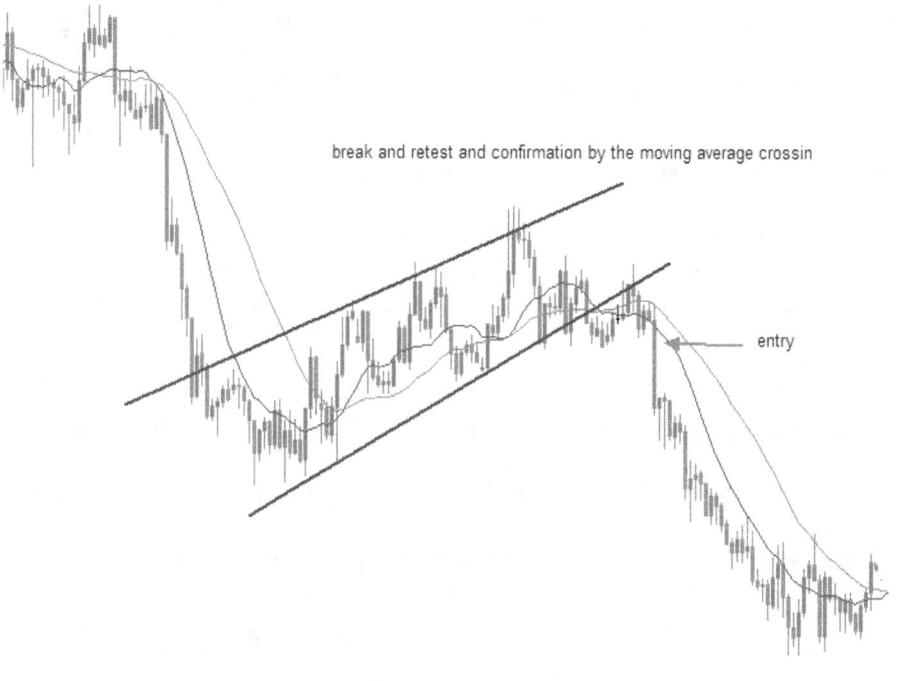

break and retest and confirmation by the moving average crossin

entry

How to Trade Swings Using Moving Averages

When swing trading, moving averages may be used in a few different ways. Below, we'll discuss three of the most often used techniques.

Determine the overall trend

The simplest use of moving averages is to determine the general trend. Probably the most popular use of MAs among traders is this one. You may rapidly determine if a market is in an uptrend, downtrend, or sideways pattern by drawing a moving average (MA) on your chart.

When the market is reaching greater highs and lower lows, an uptrend is underway. Stated differently, every subsequent high point and low point surpasses the previous one. In contrast, a downtrend causes the market to make lower highs and lower lows.

Last but not least, a sideways or range-bound market happens when the price is just bouncing between levels of support and resistance without showing any discernible direction.

Time Your Entry

Moving averages may be used to assist timing the entrance into a trade after you've determined the general trend. Let's take an example where you are examining a market that is up trending and it begins to retrace its steps towards its moving average. As long as the MA continues to act as support, this would be a good time to purchase the dip. In contrast, it can be a smart idea to sell or short an asset if it begins to rise back up towards its moving average.

Here, waiting for confirmation before making a deal is crucial. To put it another way, avoid just buying or selling whenever it crosses the moving average.

Instead, search for signs like as candlestick patterns that show the trend is still strong even after the retreat. By doing this, you may improve your chances of success and prevent false breakouts.

Exit Your Trades

You may also utilize moving averages to assist you in exiting transactions, whether they are profitable or not. For instance, if the price of an upward-trending market begins to fall below its moving average (MA), this may indicate that the trend is reversing and it is probably time to sell. In a similar vein, if the price of a commodity you hold is down trending and it begins to rise above its moving average, this may indicate that the trend is losing strength and it is time to sell.

Of course, the ideal approach to validate your exit signal is to employ MAs together with other technical indicators. For example, you may hold off on acting until the RSI indicator crosses the overbought or oversold territory.

On the other hand, you can look for candlestick patterns such as bullish or bearish reversals. How to Trade Swings Using Moving Averages

CHAPTER 6

SWING TRADING REVERSALS

Reversals are often defined as sharp price shifts that deviate from the main price trend. Reversal trading involves traders joining the opposite side of a position they are already holding in order to exit positions that are closely aligned with a trend. This occurs when a reversal is about to occur or just before it does.

Reversals may happen at any moment and are usually brought about by changes in the political, social, or economic spheres. Prices fall when an upswing takes place because purchasing interest drops. In contrast, during a declining trend, selling interest is minimal, which drives up prices.

What Are Reversal Patterns

Reversal patterns may indicate that a trend shift is likely and that neither the bulls nor the bears are in charge. There will be a halt in the present trend, after which the price will move from the other side (bear or bull).

A distribution pattern is a reversal that happens at market peaks, when there is a greater desire to sell an item than to buy it.

The reverse, known as an accumulation pattern, is a reversal that happens during market bottoms when the instrument is traded more actively in the buy than sell direction.

The most common reversal patterns are:

Head and shoulders pattern

Double top pattern

Double bottom pattern

Triple top and triple bottom pattern

Head and shoulders pattern

The head and shoulders are made up of three peaks: the shoulder, which is higher, the head, which is lower, and the shoulder, which is higher yet. By joining the two bottoms the one before and the one after the head formation the "neckline" is formed. This line is crucial since the signal is initiated by the break below.

The following figure shows both the bearish and bullish reversal patterns.

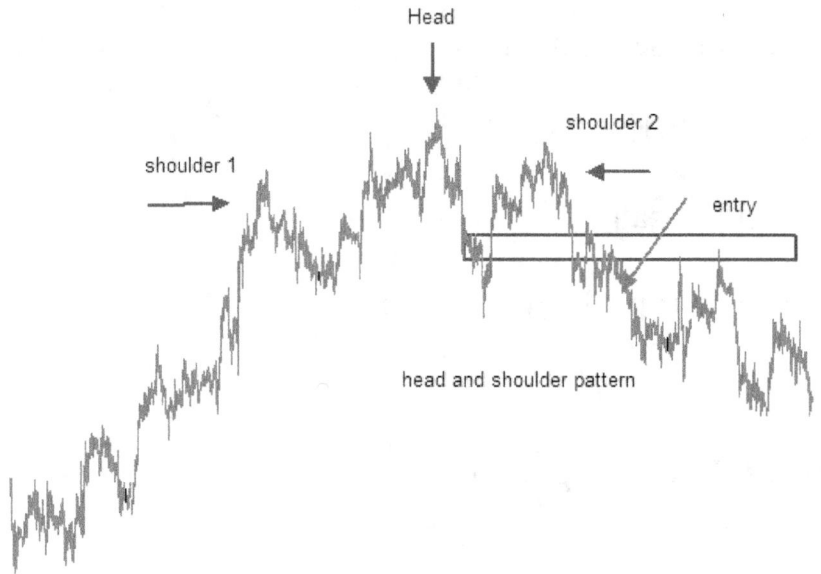

The inverse head and shoulders

Is an inverted version of the head and shoulders pattern seen in reverse charts.

Three low points make up the pattern; the head, the central low, is deeper than the two outside lows, the shoulders, which are shallower.

Usually, the completion of this pattern indicates a positive trend reversal.

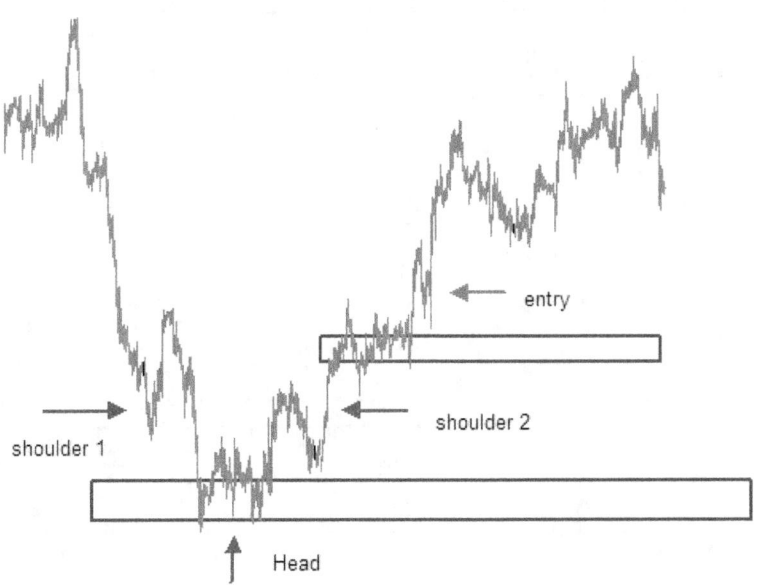

Double tops and bottoms patterns

Double tops and double bottoms show that the price has made two unsuccessful efforts to break above or below a crucial resistance or support level.

This might be a sign that the trend is losing momentum, rising purchasing pressure after a downturn that has dipped too far, or growing selling pressure following an uptrend that has entered overbought territory.

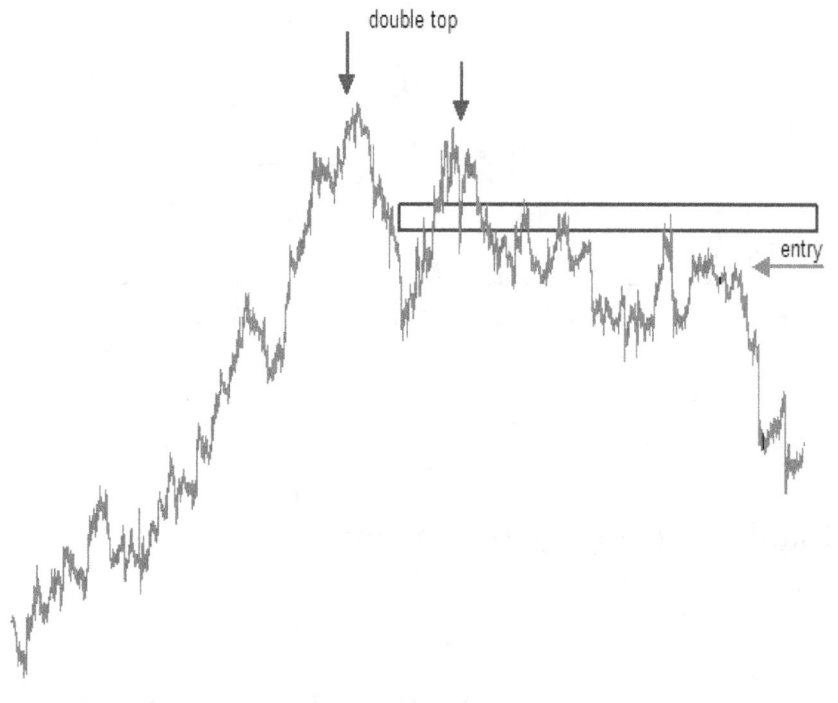

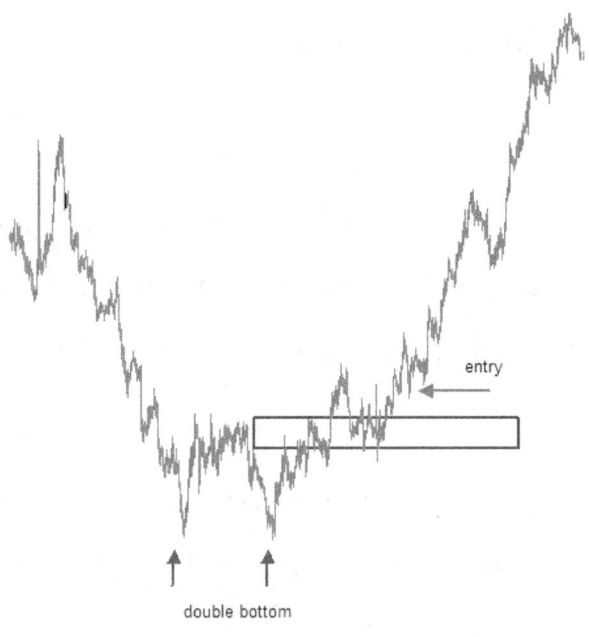

double bottom

Triple tops and triple bottoms are the names given to a related reversal pattern. Since the price did not break out twice but rather three times, indicating a greater support or resistance level, this action is significantly more potent.

Triple tops and bottoms patterns

A triple top, which is made up of three peaks that almost reached the same price, suggests that the asset's upward trend may be ending and that lower prices are likely to follow.

All time frames may see a triple top, but for the pattern to be taken into consideration, it must be part of an upward trend. The reversal pattern on this chart resembles the letter 'M' in a candlestick plot.

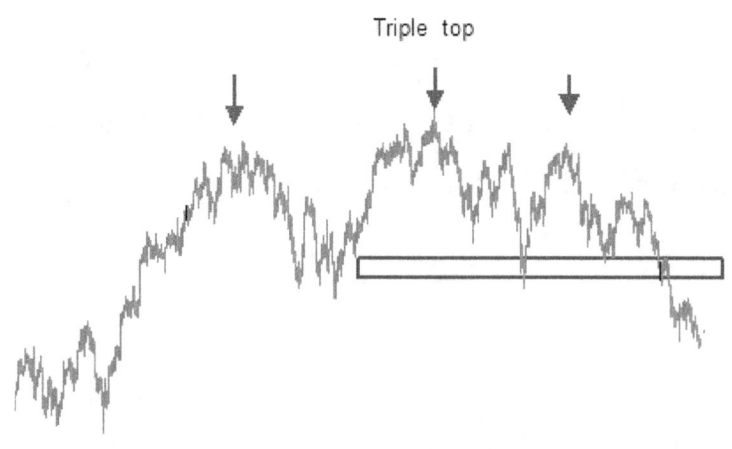

Triple top

Similar to a triple top, a triple bottom occurs after a decline and is characterized by three bottoms that coincide with a price level before the price breaks through resistance. The triple bottom chart pattern resembles the letter 'W'.

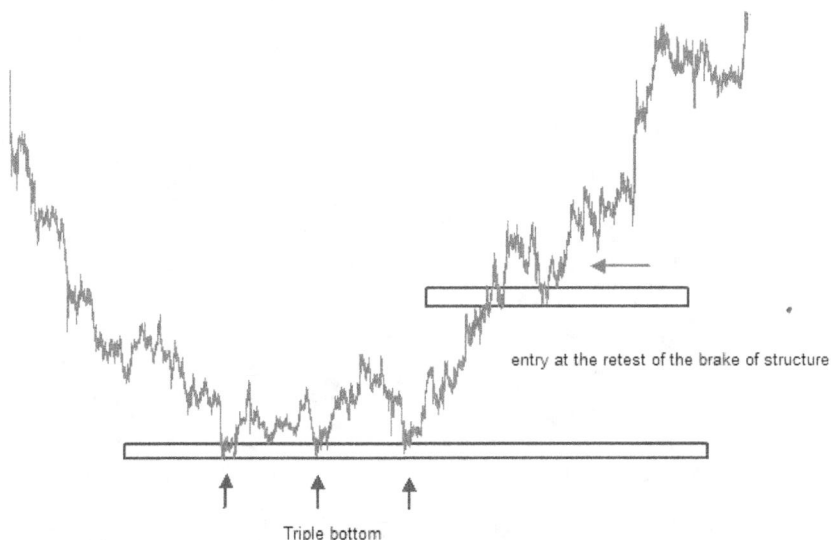

entry at the retest of the brake of structure

Triple bottom

CHAPTER 7

CONCLUSION

For those who like short-term trading but are unable to commit many hours to trading each day, swing trading is an alternate approach.

Long-term gains may be more constant with this strategy than with day trading, even if it requires a thorough grasp of technical analysis. There are hazards associated with trading, just like in any other activity. Swing traders should make sure they have a firm grasp of the technical indicators and market fundamentals that guide their trade selections, especially if they are new to the game.

A swing trader need to give careful thought to putting a stop-loss order in place in case they get unexpected information that changes their preferred path in the market.

The swing trading approach is superior to other trading methods in many ways. Even if swing trading systems are designed with a reasonable risk to reward ratio, success takes time and a great deal of patience. While trading, good money management and risk control techniques should be followed.

Trade with caution.

GET INSTANT ACCESS TO THE FREE VIDEO COURSE BY FOLLOWING THE BELOW LINK

subscribepage.io/freeforexcourse

Click or copy and paste the above link on your browser for instant access to the bonus video.

Happy Trading!